This book belongs to

_____

Dedicated to our daughters Ava and Mila who inspired us to write this story.

The day is here, the sun is shining, the **BIG BIG** world is waiting for you...

Let's get ready to explore
and keep **RONA** away too!

We wash our hands, we wear a mask...

and we stay far away.

We wear a mask when we
go outside...

Tunnels

Tunnels are fun for childrens play areas and can be used to link several structures together.

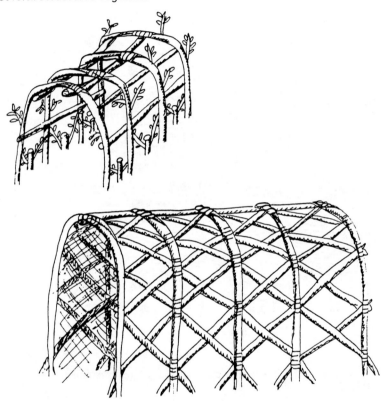

Set willow 1 foot to 1 foot 6 inches into the ground.
Put verticals in first and then join together across the top.

Then add diagonals which give strength.

Use gods eyes or string to join the intersections.
You can vary the height and width as you go along.

Woven fences.

Woven willow fences make good windbreaks as they slow the wind as it passes through. Solid wooden fences create turbulence on the leeward side.

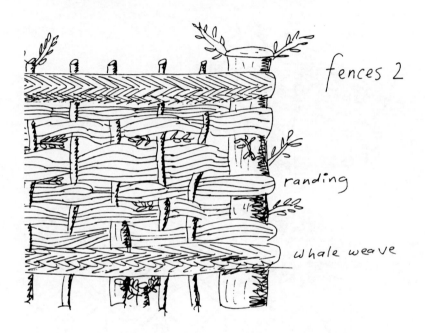

fences 2

randing

whale weave

Plant one strong 4-5 year old post every 6 feet (chesnut is very durable).

2 year old uprights every 7-10 inches.

If the structure is to grow use willow posts and occassional 2 year old uprights planted deeper to grow.

Plant willows 1ft to 1 ft 6 deep for a living fence.

14

Diagonal weave fences.

These are more open and allows a view through the fence. The diagonal weave of the fence is most suited for living structures.

Diagonal shoots interweave to create a diamond pattern.

Add uprights if you want to strengthen the fence and help to keep its shape.

A band of weaving in pairs at the top and bottom will hold it together. You can weave the tips of the diagonals into the top band to give a smooth top edge.

Arches.

An interesting feature in the garden. They can be living or non-living and you can train plants to climb·up and over. They can be incorporated into fencing.

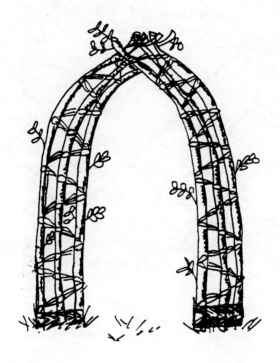

Use two or three year growth for the uprights and plant firmly into the ground.

Use one year rods for the interweaving.

Growing your own willow.

Traditionally willow was grown in osier beds in lowland areas such as the Somerset Levels but it can also be grown successfully on a small scale. Willow should be planted when it is dormant, from November to March. Cuttings need to be fresh and preferably recently cut. Don't let them dry out. Cuttings should be about 30cm long (1 foot) with 2/3 underground.

Weed control is very important, mulch mat works well and cuttings can be pushed through. Weigh it down well or it will blow away.

Rabbits can be a problem and the only effective thing to do is to fence.

Spacing can vary, smaller varieties nearer together. Approximately 45cm apart (1 1/2 foot)and 60cm (2 feet) between rows. Select varieties for colour and size, whether you intend to make baskets or large structures.

two-thirds underground

Cutting is done in the dormant period, cut right down to the stool (base) of the plant which will regrow vigorously next season. Alternatively it can be left to grow on for larger material.

Two useful texts are available from the Basketmakers Association.

"Cultivation and use of Basket Willows" by Ken Stott. A photocopy of a 1956 leaflet, 40p + SAE..
"Willow Growing" a compilation of articles by members. 40p + SAE..

<u>Places to visit:</u>

NB check opening times before making a long journey

River Parett Trail Somerset
Sculpture by Clare Wilkes at Stathe Bridge, also occasional
courses, contact the Tourist Board for info.
Tourism and Marketing Unit
South Somerset District council
Brympton Way, Yeovil
Somerset BA20 2HT 01935 462 501

Bishops Wood Environmental Ed Centre near Worcester

Henry Doubleday Research Association
Ryton Organic Gardens, Coventry
Living structures by Steve Pickup.

The Green Wood Trust
Some living willow structures. They also run courses.
Station Road, Coalbrookdale, Telford, Shropshire. TF8 7DR

Royal Horticultural Gardens, Wisley
Woking, Surrey, GU23 6QB
01483 224 234
Sculpture by Claire Wilkes and chairs by Ewen MacEwen.

Groundworks,
Rawtenstall, Lancs.
A large willow tunnel by Ian Hunter. It is in the shape of a tree
which is well established, a very good example of this type of work.

Worden Park
Leyland, Lancs.
Living arbours by Stephanie Bunn

Earthcentre
Conisborough
Near Doncaster, West Yorkshire
Large scale willow sculpture by Jim Buchanan.

Willows and Wetlands Visitor Centre
Information on the willow industry, growing and making. Visitor Centre and history.
NB. No living willow structures.

Long Ashton, near Bristol
01275 392 181
The home of the national willow collection, visits by appointment.

Ness Botanical Gardens, Cheshire
0151 353 0123
They hold a duplicate collection of the national willow collection. There are many interesting willow species around the gardens and there is a large woven willow fence with living uprights by Stephanie Bunn.

Bromley by Bow Church and Community Centre
Bruce Road
London E3
0181 980 4618
The garden is open from 9 am to 8 pm every day and has a range of willow structures by Steve Pickup.

Centre for Alternative Technology
Machynlleth, Powys SY20 9AZ
01654 703 743
A range of living willow structures made on courses run by Stephanie Bunn.

Sources of Willow

English Hurdle
Curload, Stoke St. Gregory
Taunton

Willowbank, (Steve Pickup)
PO. Box 17, Powys, SY20 8WR
 01686 430 510
Supplier of bundles of living willow for sculpture work and cuttings
of over 100 varieties for all purposes, very informative catalogue.
Also runs courses and can be commissioned for sculptures.
Website www.telecentres.com/willow-bank

PH. Coates and Sons.
Meare Green Court, Stoke St. Gregory,
NR. Taunton Somerset TA3 6HY
01823 490 249
Living willow available February to April.. Collection only.

EM & HJ Lock
Locklease
Thorney Road, Kingsbury Episcopi,
NR. Martock, Somerset TA12 6BQ
01935 823 338
Suppliers of living and non-living willow

Wally's Willows
C/o Devonshire House
Finsthwaite, Ulverston, Cumbria
SAE for list , visitors by appt.

Edgar Watts
Willow Works, Bungay
Suffolk NR35 1BW
01986 892 751
One year old rods for living willow work, cuttings also available.

Useful Addresses

Basketmakers Association
Useful information on courses, enquiries to;
King William Cottage,
Yalberton Road,
Paignton, Devon TQ4 7PE

The Cane Workshop
The Gospel Hall
Westport
Nr. Langport
Somerset TA10 0BH
Basket making tools.

Woodland Craft Supplies
Braehead Holm,
Orkney KW17 2SD
A5 SAE for catalogue of woodland craft books and tools.
Website: www.woodlandcraftsupplies.co.uk

Courses

Centre for Alternative Technology
See details earlier.

Green Wood Trust
See details earlier.

Glossary

There are many vernacular names for willow, some are; sallies, wullies, saugh, sauchan (Flora Britannica.)

Butt	Thick end or base of as rod
Coppicing	Cutting all growth back to nearly ground level
Osier	Willow variety used in basketry
Osier bed	Willow bed
Rods	One year growth
Stools	Base of plant from which rods grow.
Tip	Thin end, growth point of rod
Withy bed	Willow bed
Withy/Withies	One year old willow stem

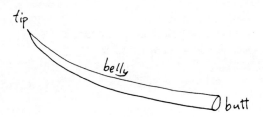

Reading.

Baskets and Basketry. Wright D. David and charles '83

Willows, the Genus Salix. Newsholme C. Batsford '92

Willows of the British Isles. Brendell T. Shire '85

Willows and Poplars. Meikle R. BSBI Handbook '84

Mommy wears a mask...
Daddy wears a mask...
and I wear a mask

We play outside in our little **bubble**...

to keep **Rona** from causing **trouble!**

Bye Bye Rona

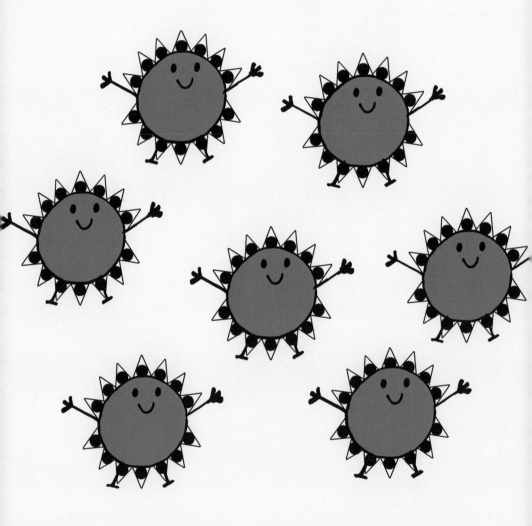

We wash our hands when we come inside...

Mommy washes her hands
Daddy washes his hands
and I wash my hands.

We do our part to stay safe everyday...

so we can stay healthy
and keep **Rona** away!

It won't be long until we can explore...

the **BIG BIG**
world that we
adore!

Bye Bye Rona

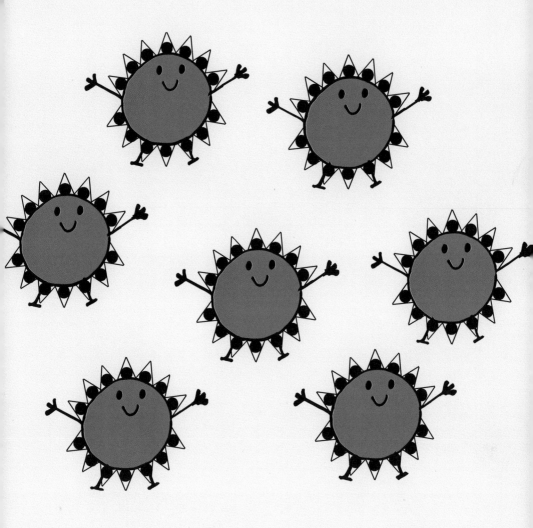

To Ruby & Dara,

I hope that you enjoy
the book.

Stay Safe!

Love Priya xxx

Printed in Poland
by Amazon Fulfillment
Poland Sp. z o.o., Wrocław

60507622R00016